NASHUA PUBLIC LIBRARY

3 4517 00203404 2

D0946907

JUV   636.1
           D

DA SILVA, MAGGIE
Horses
Grolier   c. 1

1997   97

MAY YOU ENJOY THIS BOOK

The Public Library is free to everyone living in
Nashua. You can increase its usefulness to all by
returning books promptly, on or before the "Date
Due" as stamped.

If you derive pleasure and profit from the use of
your Public Library, why not tell others about its
many services.

THE NASHUA PUBLIC LIBRARY
Nashua, N.H.

GAYLORD MG

Nature's Children

HORSES

by Maggie da Silva

Grolier Educational

FACTS IN BRIEF

JUV
636.1
D
Copy 1
NPL

Classification of the horse.

Class:	*Mammalia* (mammals)
Order:	*Perissodactyla* (odd-toed ungulates or hoofed animals)
Suborder:	*Hippomorpha*
Family:	*Equidae* (horses)
Genus:	*Equus*
Species:	*Equus caballus*

World Distribution. Once worldwide, now one species roams Mongolia in the wild. Bands of feral mustangs also reside in western North America. Domestically throughout the world.

Habitat. Primarily grasslands.

Distinctive physical characteristics. Long neck with large wide-set eyes placed on the sides of the head. Muscular upper legs and slender lower legs ending in a single toe, or hoof.Body covered with short hair, with long coarse hairs on the mane and tail. Color varies greatly.

Habits. Live in small herds or bands in the wild and forage for food during the day.

Diet. Grasses and vegetation in the wild. Grass, grain, hay, oats, and bran in captivity.

Library of Congress Cataloging-in-Publication Data

Da Silva, Maggie, 1964-
    Horses / Maggie da Silva.
        p.   cm. — (Nature's children)
    Includes index.
    Summary: Describes the physical characteristics, behavior,
domestic types, uses, and care of horses, focusing on those found on
farms or in circuses.
    ISBN 0-7172-9074-3 (hardbound)
    1. Horses—Juvenile literature.   [1. Horses.] I. Title
II. Series.
SF302.D3 1997
599.665'5—dc21

97-5977
CIP
AC

This library reinforced edition was published in 1997 exclusively by:

 Grolier Educational

Sherman Turnpike, Danbury, Connecticut 06816

Copyright 1997 The Learning Source, Ltd. All rights reserved.

Set ISBN 0-7172-7661-9
Horses ISBN 0-7172-9074-3

Contents

*Few animals have helped people as
much as the loyal, affectionate horse.*

Many millions of years ago—long before there were people—ancestors of modern-day horses roamed the earth. These mammals (called *Hyracotherium*) were only about the size of a rabbit.

As time passed, other ancestors of the horse developed, ones more like the animals we know today. Early people hunted these wild horses for food. Then, around 2000 BC, horses were domesticated, or tamed, and used as work animals and for riding. With the help of horses, people could more easily plow fields and carry goods. And they could travel long distances at great speeds. Soon horses became an important means of labor and transportation. They also became very important in warfare.

Today most workhorses have been replaced by machines of one kind or another—cars, trucks, trains, even tractors. Still, horses are used more than ever. Now, however, they are used for recreation—riding, racing, hunting, and sports. Beyond this, horse show competitions, circuses, and rodeos draw millions of spectators all around the world.

Future generations may not need horses for work. But there is little doubt that people will still want them for fun!

The Circus

In the 1700s circuses were simply shows that displayed unusual animals, such as tigers and elephants. Over the years circus owners began to include performances featuring acrobats and clowns as well as specially trained animals.

Horses were among the first animals to be used as performers in circus acts. Riders did somersaults and handstands while their horses galloped around a ring. Horses jumped over outstretched poles with performers standing on their backs. Some riders even perched on two horses at the same time, one foot on each horse's back. A few of the most daring even jumped back and forth from one horse to the other.

If these acts sound familiar to you, you are correct. Many of the stunts that thrilled audiences hundreds of years ago are still delighting circus audiences today!

*Horses have been a part of circuses
since the 1700s.*

Calf roping is one of rodeo's great tests of skill for horse and rider.

The Rodeo

Rodeos began as informal contests between cowhands in the Wild West. In the 1800s skilled cowhands competed with each other to see who was the best at riding, roping, and other ranch jobs.

People so enjoyed watching the contests that these casual competitions soon became a thing of the past. In their place was born a colorful sport in which professional cowhands showed off their skills to enthusiastic audiences—and won prize money for their efforts.

Today rodeos have five standard events: calf roping, bull riding, steer wrestling (or bulldogging), saddle bronco riding, and bareback bronco riding. (A bronco is an unbroken horse chosen for its resistance to training.) These once were the skills that every cowhand needed in order to do the chores of the day. And, thanks to the events of the rodeo, they remain alive even in today's world of trucks, tractors, and high-tech ranching.

A Day at the Races

Horse racing is one of the oldest spectator sports of all, dating back to the seventh century BC. At first only royalty and nobility could afford these exciting events, but today just about anyone can go to the races.

Thoroughbred racing is named after a kind of English horse that was bred specifically for racing and jumping. A jockey rides the horse on a flat, oval course made of grass or dirt. Most courses are a mile (1.6 kilometers) long.

In quarter-horse racing, horses race over short distances, usually a quarter mile (0.4 kilometers) on a straightaway course with no corners or turns. Quarter horses are an especially large breed that does well in races in which speed is more important than stamina.

Other Kinds of Racing

Harness racing dates back to ancient Roman horse and chariot races. Then, teams of two, four, or even six horses pulled a heavy two-wheeled chariot. Today the sport is quite different, although the basic idea is the same.

In the modern sport a single horse pulls the driver around an oval, dirt track in a light, two-wheeled vehicle called a sulky. Different breeds of horses are used in harness racing, and there are two types of races, trotting and pacing. In pacing the front leg on one side of the horse's body and the back leg of the other side move together. In trotting, both legs on each side of the body move together.

The steeplechase, which is especially popular in Great Britain, is another form of racing. It involves jumping over a variety of obstacles and is perhaps the toughest, most dangerous of all the different kinds of racing. Its name comes from the fact that long ago, the races were run over open countryside with church steeples as landmarks.

*Polo ponies are not just fast and strong; they also
are able to turn quickly and take a lot of hard
physical contact.*

Polo

Polo is another sport that uses horses. A bit like hockey on horseback, polo players use mallets to hit a small, hard ball through a goal.

Just how polo began is uncertain, but it was widely played by British army officers in India during the 1800s. It then spread to England and to North and South America.

Polo can be played either outdoors or indoors. Outdoors, the game takes place on a grass field with goalposts at either end. In an outdoor match each team has four horses and riders on the field at a time, although each rider will use several horses during the course of a match. Indoors, where space is more limited, the game is played with teams of three players.

Polo horses are called ponies. Specially trained and smaller than standard horses, polo ponies must be able to take a lot of hard contact. They also must have great endurance and be able to change direction and speed quickly. One of the most difficult of all sports, polo is as challenging for the pony as it is for the rider.

Types of Horses

Over the years horses have been bred to have special qualities to suit particular needs. The many different breeds can be divided into three major groups: ponies, draft horses, and light horses.

Ponies, like the famous Shetland and Welsh breeds, are small horses. In the past they were used to pull carts and carriages as well as to work inside coal mines. Today, however, they are most often seen giving rides to small children. They are also a familiar sight at show competitions, where their cute appearance makes them a favorite with audiences everywhere.

Draft (or heavy) horses, like Clydesdales, shires, Suffolks, and Belgians, were traditionally used for work. Pulling plows and wagons was a specialty of these strong steeds. Although they rarely do this kind of work anymore, these horses still are a symbol of strength and labor, appearing in everything from magazines to television commercials.

Light horses—the third type—are used for racing, riding, and showing. With dozens of different breeds with many markings and colors, they are the most common of all horses—and still the most popular.

Belgian draft horses are big and strong enough to do almost any kind of work.

A Horse of a Different Color

One of the most appealing features of horses is their variety. Their beautiful, shiny coats come in a wide range of colors from black, brown, and bay (reddish brown) to chestnut, dun (grayish brown), white, and golden.

Some horses have eye-catching patterns and markings. Dapple grays, for example, are gray with black hairs in circular patterns. Piebald horses, on the other hand, have black and white splotches on their bodies. Roan horses are even more striking. Their coats have a mixture of white and dark colors so that they actually look red or even blue!

Even solid-color horses are seldom plain. They may have white markings near the feet (called stockings) or wide, white stripes down the face (called blazes). Thinner markings (called stripes) and spots on the forehead (stars) also are common.

A herd of horses can be one of the most colorful sights there is.

The Morgan horse is one of the most famous of all North American breeds.

Light Horse Breeds

Light horse breeds are among the best known in North America, with names that echo through history, stories, and song. Although many light breeds originally were used for work, they now have been adapted to sport and recreation.

The most familiar North American horse of all is the American saddle horse. A mixture of several different breeds (including the thoroughbred), the saddle horse is as light and graceful as it is strong and fast. Not surprisingly, the American saddle horse is today's top choice for both riding and for shows.

One of the most famous of all North American breeds, the Morgan horse traces its history back to a New England stallion owned by Justin Morgan. For years Morgan horses were a familiar sight in American towns and cities, where they pulled carriages, buses, and even trolleys. They also were found on family farms, where they were used as both saddle horses and work horses.

The Tennessee walking horse was originally bred to carry riders over the rolling farmland of Tennessee. Its ancestors include the thoroughbred, the American saddle horse, and the Morgan. Their bloodlines combine to make the Tennessee walking horse especially fast and elegant.

Thoroughbreds

Some people think a thoroughbred is any purebred horse. But the thoroughbred is actually a special breed of running horse, with a slim body, a delicate head, broad chest, and short back. A typical thoroughbred is very fast, with a long, powerful stride. Thoroughbreds also are highly intelligent, although many people consider them to be sensitive and hot tempered. But most important, thoroughbreds usually have that combination of courage, determination, and competitiveness that horse lovers call "heart."

Remarkably, all modern thoroughbreds are descended from one of three Arabian stallions. (Arabians are the oldest of all established horse breeds; they are known for being especially strong and fast for their size.)

Back in the late 1600s and early 1700s Europeans bred their own horses with these three strong male Arabians. Since then the descendants of these three horses—Darley Arabian, Godolphin Barb, and Byerley Turk—have delighted millions of people with their racing, jumping, and hunting.

*With its slim body, broad chest, and long stride,
a thoroughbred is born to run.*

Choosing a Horse

Horses are expensive to keep and require a lot of time and energy on the part of their owners. As a result, buying a horse often is a family decision. Buyers have many things to consider before making their purchase.

Choosing the right horse depends on what it is to be used for: pulling, pleasure riding, competition, or showing. Some people prefer a specific breed or want a horse of a certain size.

Some buyers prefer stallions, male horses. These animals are big and strong, but they also can be temperamental and difficult to control. Other people find that they are more comfortable with the more peaceful personalities of geldings. (Geldings are male horses that have been neutered.) Still other people find that they have good personal "chemistry" with mares, or female horses. In the long run, however, the most important thing is for the horse and rider to get along well together.

Choosing a horse often is a family decision.

Boarding

Some people have room to keep a horse on their own property. Many people, however, do not. Instead, they board their horses at a stable.

Whether the horse is at home with its owner or boarded at a stable, it should have both a pasture or corral for exercise and a stall for shelter. A horse's stall should be at least ten feet by ten feet (three meters by three meters) square, which is large enough for the horse to lie down, get up, and turn around comfortably. The walls should be wood, and the floor, clay or sand. The floor should be covered with at least four inches of bedding (hay, straw, or wood shavings) to soak up moisture and to make a clean, dry bed.

Shelves are needed to hold hay and grain. These shelves should be at heights that are comfortable for a horse to reach when it eats. Water must be available at all times, day and night.

All horses need to get regular exercise.

Tack and Tools

A stable is full of equipment and supplies. To begin with, there is the riding equipment itself. Called tack, it includes a bridle, a saddle, and a halter.

The rider uses the bridle to control the horse. It has two parts. The first is a metal bit that fits into the horse's mouth and rests under the tongue. The second is the leather reins that are attached to the bit.

The rider sits on a saddle, which fits the horse comfortably and securely. Saddles are attached with straps that reach under and around the horse's belly. There are two basic kinds of saddles: English and western. English saddles are gently rounded, with a seat that is almost flat. A western saddle has a deep seat. It rises high in front and back, with a saddle horn directly in front of the rider.

The halter is what the horse wears when it is not wearing a bridle. It is a series of leather straps—with no bit—that go on the horse's head. A rope (called a lead line) can be attached to the halter to lead the horse around.

All riders need to understand how to use and care for their horse's tack.

Diet and Nutrition

Horses are herbivores, which means they eat no meat, only plant foods. Horses love grass, and they will nibble on it all day long if they are in a pasture. Grass is good for horses, as long as it is fresh and has not been sprayed with any chemicals.

Even the freshest, greenest grass, however, does not provide enough nutrition for most horses. Horses, especially working horses, need additional food—either hay (dried grass) or feed made from different types of grain. Oats, bran, and corn are the three types of grain that horses usually eat.

Supplements such as linseed meal, which is good for a horse's digestion and coat, may also be added to the food. All horses need salt, too, especially in hot weather. A salt block can be left in the horse's stall or out in the pasture.

Between-meal snacks, such as pieces of carrots and apples, should not be forgotten. When fed by hand, these are more than treats—they are rewards for good behavior and tokens of friendship.

Hay is an important part of most horse's diet.

Horse Behavior

Horses have very sharp senses, and their sense of hearing is the sharpest of all. A horse's ears can pick up the slightest noise.

A horse's ears are so sensitive, in fact, that they can even tell you what mood the horse is in. When a horse's ears are pointed back, the animal is angry or frightened. Ears pointed forward show interest and curiosity. One ear going each way shows uncertainty.

Horses are territorial animals that will defend their turf against any perceived threat. Males are more likely to fight than females. They may rear up on their hind legs, stab with their front hooves, or sometimes even bite.

Fights between horses, though, are not very common. By nature horses are herd animals. That means they are loyal and affectionate to other horses in their group, and they will often nuzzle and groom each other. These are the emotions and qualities that through time and training, horses can eventually transfer to their owners and riders.

Horses often will nuzzle and groom one another.

Handling and Horsemanship

How a horse is treated has a lot to do with the way it acts. Proper handling and good horsemanship on the part of the rider can usually make for a calm, predictable animal.

Any unexpected, loud noises or quick motions can make a horse feel nervous and jittery. Usually, though, a horse can be calmed down if it is talked to in a gentle, soothing voice.

There are certain "rules of the road" that can help riders keep their horses calm. To begin with, riders always should approach a horse either from its front or from its left side. This is simply because horses are trained to expect people to come from these directions.

When they are in groups, riders should give plenty of room to the horses in front of them. Riders should also pass each other at a slow gait. Otherwise, a horse may take off and start to race! One experience with a runaway horse will teach any rider the importance of this valuable lesson.

In groups, horses and riders give each other plenty of room.

Grooming

Horses need to be thoroughly groomed at least once a day. This improves the flow of the animal's blood. It also helps the horse's muscles and gives it a beautiful, shiny coat. As an added benefit, it gives the groomer a chance to check—and treat—the animal for any cuts, scratches, and scrapes.

Every part of a horse is groomed, from its hooves to its nose. First, the horse is rubbed all over with a cloth to get rid of dirt and dust. Then, its face and lower legs are stroked with a soft brush. The final step is to use a special currycomb and rough brush on the whole horse.

Horses' feet get a lot of attention. Every little rock or piece of hard dirt is picked out of the horse's hoof with a hoof pick. If a horse's feet aren't cleaned thoroughly every day, the horse may favor one leg over another and grow lame.

The real work, though, is mucking out (cleaning) the stall. The bedding must be removed and the stall shoveled out and cleaned every day. Then, the bedding is replaced with clean, fresh hay.

Taking care of a horse is a lot of work. But many horse owners think that grooming and mucking out are small prices to pay for the pleasures that come with owning such a wonderful animal.

Every part of a horse has to be washed and brushed, from its hooves to its nose.

Learning how to properly mount a horse is always an important step.

Learning to Ride

In movies and on television riding a horse looks easy. But learning to ride takes practice and patience. There is a lot for new riders to do before riding becomes second nature.

First, new riders must learn all about the horse's tack—how it fits on the horse, how to use it, and how to keep it in top condition. Next comes mounting and dismounting. Getting on a horse may look easy, but it actually is something that requires a lot of effort and practice.

Mounting actually has four steps. First, the rider stands on the horse's left side and puts his or her left foot in the stirrup. Next, the rider stands straight up, pulling up with his or her hands, which are on the top of the saddle. Finally, the rider swings the right foot over the top of the saddle and lowers it into the right stirrup.

Balance is one of the most important skills a new rider must learn. Experienced riders do not grip the horse with their legs. Instead, they keep their body's center of gravity directly over the horse's center of gravity. This makes both the horse and the rider more comfortable.

Exercise and Gait

Horses need regular exercise to stay in good shape. Responsible owners make sure their horses are ridden every day if possible.

Experienced riders warm up a horse with a nice long walk. Then they give the horse a good run for exercise. Finally, horse and rider take a slow walk home to cool off. Bringing a hot, sweaty horse back to the stable is considered very bad form.

Riders pay close attention to the animal's gait, which is the way it moves forward. Horses have three natural gaits: a walk, a trot, and a gallop. Most horses also are taught to canter. (A canter is a slow, rolling gallop.) Other horses, like the Tennessee walking horse, are taught very special gaits that are a part of the tradition of that particular breed.

Exercise time is always a good opportunity for a horse to practice its gaits.

The Veterinarian

Like most animals horses need attention from a veterinarian for everything from regular checkups to the treatment of serious injuries or diseases.

A horse checkup is not so different from what a doctor gives a human patient. The vet examines the horse's eyes, ears, lungs, intestines, and heart. After that it is time to check the horse's temperature as well as its legs and feet. The vet also sees that the horse's teeth are properly aligned.

When a horse has a cut, the vet will clean the wound and dress it. Sometimes the horse receives antibiotics to prevent infection.

Many horses go lame at one time or another in their lives. When this happens, the vet first finds out exactly where the horse is injured by gently squeezing the horse's hurt leg all over until the animal flinches. That shows the area in which the leg is hurt. X rays are then used to determine whether there is a broken bone. If there is, the vet sets the horse's leg in a cast, and the horse will have to rest it for several months.

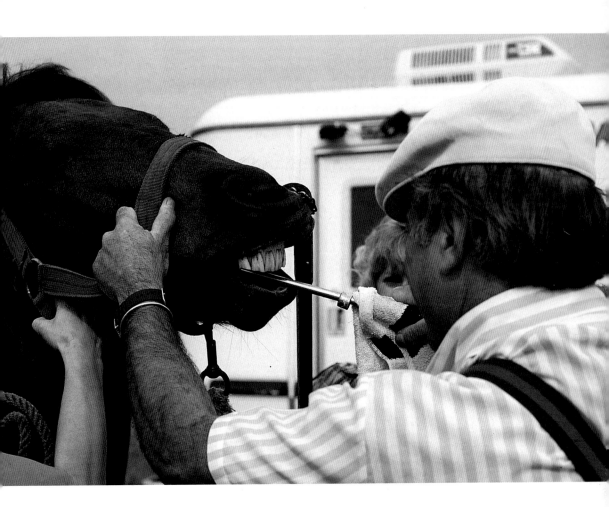

*Vets look at horse's teeth carefully
during checkups.*

Breeding

When a mare is two or three years old, she is ready to mate. A stallion can mate at about 18 months of age.

Although mares are pregnant for 11 to 12 months, the actual birth process only takes about half an hour. The foal, or baby, usually is born with its front feet first. Then it rests quietly for about 10 or 15 minutes before trying to stand. As soon as it can get up on its four feet, the foal will start nursing. Within a few hours the foal is able to run around on its long legs.

Horses will mate all year round, and foals are born in all four seasons. But no matter when a foal is born, its official birthday is the first day of the January after its birth. So all horses actually share the same birthday!

Growing Up

For their first six months yearlings live on their mother's milk, along with a little grain and a few nibbles of grass and clover. The reason for this is that it is impossible for the foal—with its long legs and short neck—to get its mouth down to the ground.

Once the foal is able to reach down to the grass, it is weaned, or taken away from its mother and her milk. To do this, the mare is moved to another stall, away from the foal. Fully weaned males are called colts; females are called fillies.

Horses grow at a fairly slow pace. In fact, they are not considered fully mature until they are seven years old. In spite of this, colts officially become known as stallions when they are four years old; fillies become mares at the same age.

Showing

People have enjoyed horse shows for centuries. The most famous riding competition, of course, is the Olympics, in which riders compete in dressage (dress-AHJ), show jumping, and other contests.

In dressage a horse performs exact, difficult, and complicated maneuvers. To do them well, the horse must be calm, balanced, and obedient. It also must be intelligent and courageous.

Jumping is quite different. Here horses run an obstacle course, going around and over fences, hedges, and even ponds or streams. Jumping horses are trained to approach obstacles with control and intelligence, making important decisions about when to jump all on their own. Scoring is done in points, with horses given penalties each time they touch or knock down an obstacle.

Jumpers go through a great deal of training so that they will be able to approach obstacles with experience and confidence. After all, even the slightest mistake can lead to a penalty—or an accident for the horse and rider.

Competitions can involve everything from dressage to show jumping.

Horses in Legend and Literature

Over the years horses have appeared in countless tales and stories. The myths of ancient Greece, in particular, are filled with great horses, from the winged, flying horse Pegasus to the Centaur, which was supposed to be half man and half horse.

In modern times authors have created many famous books in which horses are the main characters. One of the best known is *Black Beauty*, written by Anna Sewell. Other famous horse books include *National Velvet*, which tells the story of a young girl who races her horse in the famous Grand National race, and *The Black Stallion*, Walter Farley's story of a wild horse and its racehorse descendants. All of these have become classic tales, enjoyed for their adventure and for their deep understanding and love for horses.

Words to Know

Bronco   A wild, unbroken horse.

Currycomb   A comb with metal teeth, used for grooming horses.

Gait   The way a horse moves forward; the three most common gaits are a walk, a trot, and a gallop.

Jockey   A person who rides a horse in a race.

Mammal   A warm-blooded animal that gives birth to live young rather than eggs.

Rodeo   A group of contests in which riders and ropers compete using the skills of cowhands of the Old Wild West.

Steed   A horse.

Sulky   A light, two-wheeled vehicle in which a driver sits and commands a harness-racing horse.

Tack   Equipment used in riding a horse.

Thoroughbred   A horse descended from one of three Arabian stallions; usually a horse used for racing. Thoroughbreds have been bred with other types of horses to produce such breeds as the American saddle horse and the Tennessee walking horse.

X rays   Special rays that allow medical personnel to see the outlines of bones and internal organs.

Yearling   A horse that is under one year in age.

INDEX

Cover Photo: Jane Williams (Unicorn Stock Photos)
Photo Credits: Norvia Behling (Behling & Johnson Photography), pages 4, 22, 26, 29; 31, 35, 41, 45; Shirley Haley (Top Shots), pages 18, 39; Paulette Johnson (Behling & Johnson Photography), page 36; Lynn M. Stone, pages 15, 21; SuperStock, Inc., pages 7-8, 12, 17, 33; Jane Williams (Unicorn Stock Photos), page 25.